A Comprehensive Guide
to AWS Security Hub

Table of Contents

Chapter 1. Introduction

Welcome to our Special Report: "A Comprehensive Guide to AWS Security Hub." Navigating the world of cloud security can be a daunting task, especially for companies large and small that depend on AWS for their infrastructure. This guide is designed to simplify that process by providing a thorough understanding of AWS Security Hub. Don't fret if the realm of cybersecurity seems challenging; this report is geared to meet people where they are in their technological journey. From the essential tenets of AWS security management to advanced security measures, you'll find the information packed in this guide invaluable. Whether you're a seasoned IT professional or a novice at cloud computing, this robust report removes the complexity and delivers the expertise you need to secure your AWS infrastructure efficiently. Curious to uncover the secrets of AWS Security Hub? Look no further and take a step towards securing your future within the AWS cloud landscape.

Chapter 2. Introduction to AWS Security Hub

Before diving into the complexities of AWS Security Hub, let's take a definitive look at what it is and what it sets out to achieve.

Amazon Web Services (AWS), the world's most comprehensive and widely adopted cloud platform, offers a suite of services and tools that aid in maintaining security standards. AWS Security Hub is one such service, offering a comprehensive view of high-priority security alerts and the overall security status of AWS resources.

2.1. A Brief Overview

AWS Security Hub serves as a centralized hub for security data collection and consolidation. It aids organizations that have expansive AWS ecosystems by eliminating the complexities of managing multiple, disparate security services. AWS Security Hub lays its foundation on three principal functionalities: aggregating security findings, analyzing these findings across AWS accounts, and automating security tasks with plays.

One perhaps might think of AWS Security Hub as the conductor of an orchestra, where each musician plays a different instrument — in this case, each weapon in your cybersecurity arsenal is an instrument and the Security Hub is responsible for orchestrating harmonious security operations.

2.2. A Closer Look at the Functionalities

Let's dissect further each of these functionalities:

1. Aggregating Security Findings

As AWS landscapes grow and evolve, so do the corresponding security metrics and alerts. AWS Security Hub gathers security data from various AWS services and partner solutions, allowing you to manage all of these diverse findings from a single, unified interface. The unified view simplifies the process and enables security teams to discern patterns and correlations that they would otherwise miss when analyzing each service independently.

1. Analyzing Across AWS Accounts

In the face of increasing security threats, companies frequently manage multiple AWS accounts to segment and secure their data. AWS Security Hub enables analysis across multiple AWS accounts, providing an aggregated view of all findings. This cross-account view helps in detecting any irregularities and patterns that an isolated, single-account view may overlook.

1. Automating Security Tasks with Plays

To combat the dynamic and rapidly evolving world of cybersecurity threats, AWS Security Hub is equipped to automate security tasks using AWS Security Hub Plays. These Plays, based on AWS Step Functions (AWS's serverless workflow service), allow security teams to define automatic remediation and responses to specific findings. This automation not only saves resources but also counteracts threats in a timely and efficient manner.

2.3. Benefits of AWS Security Hub

With the power of AWS Security Hub, you can harness a gamut of benefits. Some of these benefits include:

1. Increased Visibility: With AWS Security Hub, you get a detailed and consolidated view of security alerts and compliance status

across your AWS environment. This increased visibility helps in identifying potential threats and addressing them proactively.

2. Enhanced Efficiency: AWS Security Hub aggregates and normalizes security findings from various AWS services and AWS partner solutions in one place. This unified view enhances efficiency and facilitates centralized security management.

3. Improved Compliance: AWS Security Hub automatically runs continuous, account-level configuration and compliance checks based on industry standards and best practices, helping organizations maintain an improved compliance status.

4. Streamlined Workflow: By automating responses to specific findings with AWS Security Hub Plays, the service helps in streamlining your security workflow and allowing your security team to focus on more critical matters.

2.4. Understanding Security Findings

One of AWS Security Hub's unique features is its approach to what it calls 'findings'. A finding is a potential security issue discovered by one of the AWS services or AWS partner solutions.

AWS Security Hub provides a detailed view of each finding, which includes information like:

1. The AWS resource associated with the issue.

2. The last time the issue was observed.

3. The severity of the issue.

4. The status of the issue.

With thousands of potential findings flooding in every day, AWS Security Hub consolidates and categorizes these findings into a few stereotypical types.

2.5. AWS Security Hub - Compliance Checks

In addition to managing security findings, AWS Security Hub also monitors your AWS accounts' compliance status. It does this by continuously running a set of compliance checks that are based on industry standards and best practices.

AWS Security Hub uses a framework of security standards, where a security standard comprises several controls, and each control has multiple rules. Each rule is a compliance check.

Compliance checks are invaluable to maintaining optimal security within your AWS landscape. It's like having a security guard who never sleeps, relentlessly ensuring that your AWS configurations align with best practices and security protocols.

2.6. Partnering with AWS Security Hub

While AWS Security Hub ingests data from other AWS security services, its operational capabilities extend beyond just AWS-owned tools. You can add a significant layer of versatility to your security operations by integrating AWS Security Hub with a wide range of third-party security solutions via AWS's Security Finding Format (ASFF).

With this, we wrap up the introduction to AWS Security Hub. As we move forward, this guide will delve deeper into the various facets of operationalizing AWS Security Hub and how it can become a pivotal part of your cybersecurity operations.

AWS Security Hub, when harnessed to its full potential, can drastically simplify and enhance your AWS security setup. By consolidating alerts, providing invaluable insights, and automating responses, you can rest easy knowing your AWS resources are guarded effectively. This peace of mind allows your organization to focus on what's important - growing and innovating within the cloud.

And as you embark on this journey of securing your AWS environment, remember that security isn't merely an automated process but a culture. At its foundation, AWS Security Hub aims to foster that culture in your organization, making security everyone's responsibility.

Chapter 3. Why AWS Security Hub: Advantages and Use Cases

As a centralized service that bolsters the security and compliance of your organization, AWS Security Hub plays an invaluable role in cloud security management. It's designed to provide comprehensive visibility into your security and compliance status across multiple AWS accounts, in a single dashboard. Having a centralized overview allows you to continuously monitor your environment using automated compliance checks and detect threats in real-time, thereby helping you to maintain a robust control over the security of your AWS solution.

3.1. Overview of AWS Security Hub

One advantage of AWS Security Hub is that it consolidates, organizes, and prioritizes your security alerts or findings from various AWS services, such as Amazon GuardDuty, Amazon Inspector, and Amazon Macie, as well as from AWS Partner solutions. When managing large workloads in the cloud, it becomes increasingly difficult to keep track of notifications generated by various services. That's where AWS Security Hub comes handy as it makes the task much simpler by bringing everything together.

Amazon's Security Hub operates using an AWS-native system. This facilitates seamless integration with other AWS services and tools. Not only does this simplify your overall operations via native solutions, but it also provides a platform for streamlined security management.

Another strength of AWS Security Hub is its ability to carry out automated security checks based on industry standards and best practices, such as the Center for Internet Security (CIS) AWS Foundations Benchmark. The service provides scorecards along with a detailed explanation of failed compliance checks, enabling your security team to understand, rectify and improve your overall security posture.

3.2. Streamlined Security Management

AWS Security Hub facilitates proactive and streamlined security management. It reduces the operational overhead by automatically aggregating alerts and findings from multiple services into prioritized, actionable items. No longer do teams need to switch between different consoles to manage and respond to security events, thereby saving precious time and effort.

Moreover, reactive measures to security incidents can often be inefficient and delayed. Security Hub helps transform reactive steps to proactive measures. It collects data across your AWS accounts, analyzes the information to identify potential threats, and prioritizes findings to put the most critical threats on top, enabling security teams to address risks proactively.

This centralization of security findings also ensures that suspicious activities are not buried under a pile of other alerts and hence unnoticed. By organizing the alerts based on their severity and aligning them with the AWS best practices, AWS Security Hub highlights the most potential security threat at a given point of time for organizations to mitigate.

3.3. Facilitating Compliance

One of the critical responsibilities for any corporate is to adhere to regulations and industry norms. AWS Security Hub aids in facilitating compliance adherence in various ways. First, it continually checks your environment against a selected set of compliance controls. This results in quick identification of areas where your account does not adhere to certain compliance standards, allowing you to take corrective action swiftly.

Security Hub also provides detailed compliance reports that can be downloaded for your records. These reports contain per-resource scoring of your security settings, as well as recommendations for enhancing your security posture. This allows you to address compliance issues more proactively and helps you demonstrate your commitment to stringent security standards.

3.4. Use Cases of AWS Security Hub

The dynamic nature of AWS Security Hub equips it to handle various scenarios based on the most pressing requirements of your organization, be it security threat detection, compliance checks or simply managing the security health of your AWS landscape.

1. **Security Remediation**: With AWS Security Hub, you can identify security vulnerabilities across your environments, understand their impact, and take steps to mitigate them. The service provides findings that result from a detailed analysis of data, helping you understand and rectify the vulnerabilities.

2. **Compliance Assurance**: AWS Security Hub helps you maintain a pulse on your compliance status. It performs automated checks based on standards like CIS AWS Foundations Benchmark to ensure that your accounts follow the recommended AWS best practices. The continuous monitoring helps maintain the compliance posture of your organization.

3. **Centralized Security Monitoring**: Organizations with multiple AWS accounts or a large number of services often suffer from alert fatigue. AWS Security Hub solves this problem with centralized security monitoring, eliminating the need to switch

between different consoles for managing security findings.

4. **Threat Detection**: The Security Hub integrates with services like Amazon GuardDuty for intelligence-driven threat detection. It collects, analyzes, and prioritizes potential threats, enabling you quickly address the security risks.

Collectively, the AWS Security Hub serves as an all-in-one solution that allows organizations to manage their security and compliance simultaneously. It's an essential tool for organizations looking to protect their AWS cloud investments actively. It amalgamates features of various services, automates the process of security checks, acts as a unified dashboard, and, most importantly, transforms the way your organization manages cloud security efficiently and effectively.

Chapter 4. Understanding AWS Security Standards, Protocols and Compliance

To begin the journey into the comprehensive world of AWS Security Hub, comprehending the strengths and fundamentals of Amazon's approach to security is key. AWS operates infrastructure at a global scale with an unparalleled focus on security.

AWS incorporates a variety of stringent security measures, which include a broad selection of articulated standards, strict protocols, and adherence to a wide range of compliance programs. These aspects form the foundation for ensuring secure data handling and providing reliable services to its users.

4.1. AWS Security Standards

AWS adheres to a defined set of security standards and practices, some of which are:

1. Data Encryption: AWS ensures that your data is protected both in transit and at rest. AWS provides a host of options for data encryption, allowing you to choose the one that best fits your security strategy.

2. Identity and Access Management (IAM): AWS IAM enables you to manage access to AWS services and resources securely. You can create and manage AWS users and groups, and use permissions to allow and deny their access to AWS resources.

3. Multi-Factor Authentication (MFA): AWS also employs MFA solutions for increased account security. MFA invites users to present two or more separate identities to affirm access.

4. Infrastructure Security: AWS data centers employ innovative

architectural and engineering approaches to physical security to provide world-class protection for their servers, with a direct correlation to the various compliance standards.

4.2. AWS Security Protocols

Aside from the stringent security standards, AWS utilizes protocols that ensure secure interactions between AWS and your local environment. These protocols are important to ensure the right entities access the right resources at the right time, securely.

1. Secure Socket Layer/Transport Layer Security (SSL/TLS): These protocols are used for secure, authenticated communication between AWS services. By encrypting the data in transit, it mitigates the potential for data tampering or unauthorized access.

2. AWS Signature Version 4: Is a cryptographic protocol for secure access to your AWS services. It authenticates every request sent to AWS, ensuring that only authorized users (those with the right access keys) can access your resources.

3. Amazon Virtual Private Cloud (VPC): A logically isolated section of AWS where you can launch resources in a defined virtual network. It allows secure communication with your data center using industry-standard encrypted IPsec VPN connections.

4.3. AWS Compliance Programs

At the heart of Amazon's approach to auditing its security practices lies a wide range of compliance programs. They have established numerous certifications with third parties and governing bodies, helping ensure AWS's alignment with different legislative and industry standards across regions and sectors.

1. International Organization for Standardization (ISO): AWS

compliance includes the broadest selection of ISO certifications, which serve to standardize preventative information security measures.

2. The Service Organization Control (SOC): AWS maintains the SOC 1, 2, and 3 reports demonstrating how they maintain the security, availability, and confidentiality of the systems that store, process, and transmit customer data.

3. Payment Card Industry Data Security Standard (PCI DSS): AWS complies with this standard. Hence, it safeguards the cardholder's data across ecommerce transactions and reduces credit card fraud.

4. Health Insurance Portability and Accountability Act (HIPAA) compliant: AWS safeguards patient privacy through supporting HIPAA-compliant health tech companies.

5. Federal Information Security Management Act (FISMA) compliant: AWS provides FISMA-compliant cloud services, supporting government agencies' digital transformation.

In closing, understanding the various standards, protocols, and compliance programs adhered to and put forth by AWS can highly inform your navigation through Amazon Security Hub. Once you have a firm understanding of these components, you're well on your way to mastering the Hub's tools and features to enhance the security measures in place for your AWS infrastructure.

The subsequent sections will delve into more critical topics, such as AWS Key Management Service (KMS), AWS Identity, and Access Management (IAM), the role of the Shared Responsibility Model, Security by Design, and Incident Response, among others. These concepts build upon the foundations laid herein to provide a holistic understanding of AWS Security Hub and its capabilities.

Chapter 5. Setting Up AWS Security Hub: A Step-by-Step Guide

Let's embark on the journey of setting up AWS Security Hub. It is a carefully designed process, ensuring each measure you take contributes to building an all-encompassing security shell for your AWS architecture.

5.1. Understanding AWS Security Hub

Before setting up AWS Security Hub, it's essential to have a basic understanding of what it is and why it's crucial for managing your cloud security. AWS Security Hub provides a comprehensive view of your high-priority security alerts and your compliance status across AWS accounts. It collects security data from various AWS services, helps to analyze your environment's security, and presents findings that aid in identifying potential threats.

5.2. AWS Accounts

AWS Security Hub can function with a single AWS account or multiple AWS accounts. If you have more than one AWS account, the process of setting them up with Security Hub involves defining one as a master account and others as member accounts. The main advantage here is that the master account can view and manage security findings from all accounts.

5.3. AWS Security Hub Prerequisites

Before setting up AWS Security Hub, it's essential to verify and configure prerequisites that include:

- Your AWS account must be part of AWS Organizations, and you must use the management account of your organization to enable Security Hub.

- AWS Config must be enabled for every region that Security Hub checks resources in.

- Ensure that you have the necessary IAM permissions.

- Confidence in the AWS Regions you'll use, as Security Hub is enabled for each region separately.

5.4. Enabling AWS Security Hub

With prerequisites out of the way, let's take a step towards enabling AWS Security Hub.

5.4.1. Using the AWS Management Console

Let's begin with the AWS Management Console:

1. Open the AWS Management Console.

2. Look for 'Security Hub' in the AWS Services search bar and select it.

3. Click on 'Go to Security Hub'.

4. Select the settings wheel at the top-right and then choose 'Enable AWS Security Hub'.

5. Read and accept the service-linked role agreement by selecting 'Enable'.

5.4.2. Using the AWS CLI

Now let's confige Security Hub through the AWS CLI:

1. Open the AWS CLI on your local machine.

2. Run the following command in the CLI:

```
aws securityhub enable-security-hub --no-enable-default
-standards
```

This command enables the hub without enabling the compliance checks, keeping it clean until you decide which standards to apply.

5.5. Configuring AWS Security Hub Standards

After setting up AWS Security Hub, the next step is to configure the security standards. AWS Security Hub Supports multiple security standards, including:

- CIS AWS Foundations Benchmark

- AWS Foundational Security Best Practices

- PCI DSS

5.5.1. Using the AWS Management Console

To configure standards in AWS Management Console:

1. Go to the AWS Management Console and open Security Hub.

2. Choose 'Settings'.

3. Select the 'Standards' tab.

4. Choose the standard you wish to enable and select 'Enable

standard'.

5.5.2. Using the AWS CLI

To enable a standard via AWS CLI, run the following command:

```
aws securityhub batch-enable-standards --standards
-subscription-requests
StandardsArn=arn:aws:securityhub::<your-
region>::standard/aws-foundational-security-best-
practices/v-1.0.0
```

Replace '<your-region>' with your AWS region.

Repeat this process for all the standards you wish to enable.

5.6. Inviting and Managing Members

If you're using multiple AWS accounts, you can invite your member accounts and manage them from the master account.

5.6.1. Inviting a Member

To invite a member:

1. In the AWS Management Console, select 'Settings', and then the 'Accounts' tab.

2. Choose 'Invite Members'.

3. Type the AWS account ID or email address associated with the AWS account you wish to invite.

4. Choose 'Invite'.

5.6.2. Accepting Invitations

To accept a membership invitation:

1. In the AWS Management Console , go to the 'Membership' page.
2. Under 'Actions', select 'Accept' to join.

This concludes our expansive guide on setting AWS Security Hub. Once set up, it will provide a competitive edge to your security strategies by offering a centralized, thorough, and automated approach to safeguarding your AWS infrastructure. Happy and secure cloud computing!

Chapter 6. Exploring the AWS Security Hub Dashboard

When we begin talking about AWS Security Hub, the very starting point is always its Dashboard. The AWS Security Hub dashboard acts as the centralized hub where you can monitor and manage all security concerns related to your AWS infrastructure.

Upon logging in, you land on the AWS Security Hub dashboard. Here, a series of graphs and tables provide a comprehensive visual overview of your security posture on AWS. It represents notifications, findings from various AWS security services, compliance standards, and security scores - all in a consolidated, digestible format.

6.1. Getting Familiar with the Dashboard

To navigate the AWS Security Hub Dashboard, it's crucial to familiarize yourself with its sections. The Home page displays a summary of security alerts or "findings." The findings give valuable insight into the security issues in your AWS environment and are organized in several widgets. You can also customize these widgets according to your preference.

- Security Standards widget: This shows a brief about your compliance with the various Security Standards supported by AWS Security Hub.

- Insights widget: It highlights interesting patterns and areas of concern across the findings.

- Findings Summary widget: It illustrates the distribution of the findings based on various criteria like the severity, AWS account and more.

You can click on the individual widgets for a drilled-down view, providing granular details about the state of your security posture.

6.2. Understanding the Findings and Insights

Findings in AWS Security Hub are potential security issues detected by the product integrations you've enabled. They are generated from AWS security services like Amazon GuardDuty, Amazon Inspector, and Amazon Macie and third-party tools.

Each finding comes with an assigned severity level, ranging from Low to Critical, indicating the level of risk that the issue represents.

Insights are aggregated and sorted findings that help identify potential security issues. They can be created by filtering and grouping findings based on your needs. By effectively utilizing insights, you can track and categorize the findings that matter most to your organization.

6.3. Navigating Compliance Standards

Compliance management is an integral part of any security paradigm, including AWS. Security Hub provides a strong compliance management toolset, allowing you to enforce your security and compliance using a broad range of supported frameworks. These frameworks include CIS AWS Foundations Benchmark, PCI DSS, and others.

Clicking on the "Security Standards" section in the dashboard will lead you to a new page displaying the status of your compliance against these frameworks. This status is expressed as a percentage. Here, each control in a security standard relates to a specific recommendation in a framework, and each control has findings related to it.

Exploring these will help you identify which security controls you are lacking and those you need to enforce or improve.

6.4. Customizing Your Dashboard

The security needs of organizations vary greatly, and thus AWS Security Hub provides customization options for the dashboard. Users can choose what they want displayed by adjusting the settings in the custom actions section of the dashboard.

Custom actions allow you to take batch actions on findings by sending them to an HTTP endpoint, invoking a Lambda function, or even sending an automated response using Amazon CloudWatch Event rules. This way, you can create custom processes based on defined parameters, enabling smoother security operations within your AWS environment.

In conclusion, the AWS Security Hub Dashboard is a robust, multifaceted tool that provides a panoramic view of your AWS security status. From insights and findings related to your security posture to the details of the compliance standards, it offers the necessary leverage to manage, navigate and contour your security strategies effectively. This is your main command center for security operations in your AWS infrastructure, designed to provide you with the control and information needed to secure your assets adequately.

Chapter 7. Mastering AWS Security Hub Features

Before we dive into the robust features of AWS Security Hub, it is important to understand the basic premise of this platform. AWS Security Hub provides a comprehensive view of your high-priority security alerts and compliance status across AWS accounts. There are two main functional areas that AWS Security Hub covers — security standards and insights.

7.1. Security Standards

Security Standards in AWS Security Hub provide automated security checks based on well-known security best practices and industry standards your company may want to follow. There are several standards currently supported with more being added over time.

1. AWS Foundational Security Best Practices

2. Center for Internet Security (CIS) AWS Foundations Benchmark

3. Payment Card Industry Data Security Standard (PCI DSS)

4. AWS HIPAA

After you enable a security standard, AWS Security Hub automatically runs its security checks as part of that standard and lists all of those checks on the Security Standards page.

7.2. Insights

Insights are correlation rules that help in sorting and filtering findings. Security Hub provides a set of managed insights that you can't modify or delete. You can also create your own custom insights by grouping together findings that share specific attribute values.

Insights provide a count of the grouped findings, and they dynamically update to reflect the results of the most recent Security Hub ingestion and aggregation process.

Now, let's explore the features one by one that will be mastered in the AWS Security Hub.

7.3. Centralized Security and Compliance Views

AWS Security Hub has collected, organized, and prioritized your security findings from multiple AWS services and AWS Partner solutions. You can filter, aggregate, and visualize these findings based on their Amazon Resource Name (ARN), tags, or AWS accounts. This has simplified security and compliance reporting, and let you focus on protecting against the threats that matter most.

7.4. Automated Security Checks

AWS Security Hub provides automated security checks based on industry standards, such as the Center for Internet Security (CIS) AWS Foundations Benchmark and the PCI DSS. You can immediately see your high-priority AWS security findings on this integrated dashboard. Additionally, Security Hub includes compliance standards to help meet specific regulatory requirements, such as HIPAA and GDPR.

7.5. Insightful Graphical Summary

AWS Security Hub's graphical summary provides helpful visualizations of security and compliance status across your AWS accounts. It gives a holistic, organized, and easily understood view of your security posture.

7.6. Continuous Compliance Checks

As part of its automated security checks, AWS Security Hub offers continuous compliance checks that align with industry standards. This means that your compliance status is not static and constantly being checked, reflected in updates Security Hub makes to your compliance status.

7.7. Integration with AWS Services and Partner Solutions

Another intriguing feature of AWS Security Hub is its seamless interoperability with other AWS Services like Amazon CloudWatch, AWS Lambda, Amazon SNS, and partner solutions like CrowdStrike, Palo Alto Networks, Anomaly, and many more. This offers organizations the flexibility to use their preferred solutions for specific security tasks without compromising on overall visibility.

7.8. Customizable Reporting

AWS Security Hub allows organizations to create custom insights that help identify trends and patterns in your security posture over time. For instance, you might create an insight that tracks how many findings of a particular type are generated each month or which resources are most frequently flagged for security incidents.

7.9. Built-in Remediation

When AWS Security Hub identifies a critical finding, it doesn't just alert you - it can also initiate remediation actions using Amazon CloudWatch Events and AWS Lambda. This automatic remediation can significantly speed up your response times to critical findings, improving your overall security posture.

AWS Security Hub is a fast, efficient, and cost-effective option for managing security and compliance across your AWS environment. The key to mastering this feature-rich service lies in understanding how to configure its features and use the insights it provides to drive proactive security measures. As part of your ongoing security management strategy, AWS Security Hub can serve as both an anchor for your security posture and a beacon, illuminating potential security issues. With this comprehensive knowledge in hand, you will have an all-round understanding of AWS Security Hub, equipped to face any challenges that may come your way in the AWS cloud realm.

Chapter 8. AWS Security Hub Best Practices and Tips

The first step towards leveraging AWS Security Hub to its highest potential is to understand and adopt the best practices and tips for maximum efficiency.

8.1. Understanding AWS Security Hub

AWS Security Hub is a centralized view that provides you with security findings across your AWS accounts. It enables you to have a comprehensive understanding of your high-priority security alerts and compliance status. The Security Hub consolidates, organizes and prioritizes your alerts, or what AWS calls findings, from multiple AWS services like Amazon GuardDuty, Amazon Inspector, Amazon Macie, AWS Firewall Manager, as well as from AWS Partner solutions.

To use AWS Security Hub, you need to enable it in each AWS region where you want to see the aggregated and organized security findings. Once turned on, Security Hub will start ingesting the findings from the integrated services.

8.2. Integrating AWS Services with Security Hub

Before diving into the best practices, one should be aware of how to integrate AWS Security Hub with other AWS services. Doing so allows the Security Hub to ingest security findings from those services. Here are the steps:

1. Enable AWS Security Hub in your account

2. Enable AWS Config in each region where the Security Hub is enabled

3. For each integrated service, you should assure that the service is also enabled in the region

If you correctly follow these steps, the integration scenario will provide a robust foundation for implementing the best practices associated with AWS Security Hub.

8.3. Regulatory Compliance Standards

AWS Security Hub supports multiple regulatory compliance standards, such as PCI DSS, CIS AWS foundations benchmark, and many more. You should regularly track your compliance score in these frameworks and work towards improving it as this score is a reflection of your overall security posture.

8.4. Prioritizing Security Findings

The AWS Security Hub presents each security finding along with some associated attributes. These attributes include Title, Description, Severity, Resources Involved and more. The 'Severity' attribute can help you prioritize these findings. It is beneficial to focus first on high severity findings and then work your way down to the less severe ones.

8.5. Set Alerts for Security Findings

You should use Amazon CloudWatch to create customized alerts when new highseverity findings are detected. These alerts can be sent using multiple channels including email, SMS, or AWS Chime and can serve to notify your security teams to act immediately.

8.6. Use Security Standards

Security Hub provides a feature called Security Standards, which is a set of pre-configured security checks based on industry and regulatory frameworks. For instance, using the AWS Foundational Security Best Practices you can check for violations of security best practices across your resources.

8.7. Performing regular audits

At the heart of any secure system is the concept of regular audits. These audits can be done using AWS Config, which provides a detailed inventory of your AWS resources and configuration, while continuously monitoring and recording your resource configurations and allowing you to automate the evaluation of recorded configurations against desired configurations.

8.8. Integrating with DevOps Lifecycle

The DevOps approach to AWS Security provides automated, continuous investment in the security of your AWS infrastructure. As part of DevOps, you can use AWS CodePipeline, together with AWS Security Hub, to check the vulnerabilities in your code before it is deployed. If the severe findings are detected, you can configure the pipeline to stop, making security an integral part of your DevOps lifecycle.

Chapter 9. Securing Access with IAM Roles and Policies

IAM roles for AWS Security Hub should be created and managed wisely. The principle of least privilege should be followed when granting permissions to Security Hub. IAM policy permissions should be reviewed regularly and outdated policies should be updated or removed.

To answer the security concern in the modern era, AWS Security Hub offers a wide range of tools and features. By following the best practices and methods mentioned above, you can significantly enhance the safety and security of your AWS infrastructures. Continuous auditing, integrating with DevOps, giving importance to regulatory standards, and securing access form a formidable wall of security around your AWS assets, making your cloud journey safe and secure.

Remember, AWS Security Hub empowers you to secure your systems, but it's ultimately the effective use of its tools and features that determine your overall security posture.

Chapter 10. Integrating AWS Security Hub with Other AWS Services

In order to best leverage the capabilities of AWS Security Hub, integrating it with other AWS services is crucial. This helps you to examine security findings in the context of other resources and workloads. This synergy not only promotes excellent security agility, but it also provides visibility into the security and compliance status of your AWS accounts ultimately leading to a more coherent and efficient security risk management.

10.1. The Mechanics of Integration

The process of integrating AWS Security Hub with other AWS services begins with first enabling AWS Security Hub in your region. Enabling Security Hub involves accepting the permissions and security configuration that AWS has defined and allows Security Hub to associate with your AWS account.

To enable Security Hub, follow these simple steps:

1. Visit the AWS Management Console.

2. Navigate to the 'Services' drop-down, and select 'AWS Security Hub'.

3. Click on 'Go to Security Hub'.

4. Accept the prompts regarding permissions and security configurations.

Once AWS Security Hub is enabled, integration with other AWS services can begin. Each AWS service offers unique integration opportunities, contributing diverse insights and findings to your security information pool.

10.2. Integrating with Amazon GuardDuty

Amazon GuardDuty is a threat detection service that continuously monitors for malicious or unauthorized behavior. Integrating this service with AWS Security Hub can provide security administrators with rich threat detection data.

To integrate GuardDuty with Security Hub:

1. Navigate to Amazon GuardDuty in the AWS Management Console.

2. Select the 'Settings' tab, and enable the 'Auto-enable' option.

3. Next, under the 'Export Findings To' option, enable 'AWS Security Hub'.

4. At last, Save changes.

With integration complete, security findings from GuardDuty will now be compiled alongside other Security Hub data, providing a comprehensive account of your security landscape.

10.3. Integrating with AWS Config

AWS Config provides a detailed inventory of your AWS resources and their current configurations, while continuously recording configuration changes. By integrating it with AWS Security Hub, you can have visibility into resource changes that may affect your security posture.

To integrate with AWS Config:

1. Navigate to AWS Config in your AWS Management Console.

2. In 'Settings', enable 'Record configuration changes'.

3. Next, in the 'Stream configuration changes and notifications to Amazon CloudWatch Events' option, select 'Yes'.

4. Finally, create an AWS Config Rule that evaluates your resources for compliance with desired configurations.

Now, AWS Config and Security Hub work together to provide panoramic visibility into your AWS landscape, allowing you to quickly make security-related decisions if your resources drift from their desired configurations.

10.4. Using Amazon CloudWatch with Security Hub

Amazon CloudWatch is a monitoring and observability service. You can use CloudWatch to collect and track metrics, collect and monitor log files, and respond to system events. Integration of CloudWatch with Security Hub allows for real-time monitoring of your security posture.

To achieve this:

1. Navigate to CloudWatch in your AWS Management Console.

2. In the 'Events' section, create a new rule.

3. For the 'Event pattern', select 'Build event pattern to match events by service'. Now, choose 'Security Hub' as the service.

4. Set up the target as a Lambda function, SNS topic, or another supported service.

5. Define the details for your target, click 'Configure details'.

6. Provide a name and description for this rule, then click 'Create'.

Through CloudWatch, you can follow real-time events related to your security posture and respond quickly to any deviations or anomalies.

10.5. Conclusion

Integration of AWS Security Hub with other AWS Services lays the foundation for a more complex and robust AWS security architecture by providing a more thorough and comprehensive understanding of your security landscape. It allows for real-time visibility into potential threats, unauthorized behavior, configuration drifts, and overall system health, thereby empowering you to respond quickly to evolving security events. As AWS continues to grow and evolve, ensuring these integrations are in place and functioning as intended will continue to be an essential part of managing your security in the AWS cloud.

Chapter 11. Dealing with Security Threats in AWS: Roles of Security Hub

The realm of cybersecurity is a continuously evolving battlefield where defenders constantly ward off malicious entities intending to compromise system integrity and privacy. While AWS infrastructures are secure, a concrete understanding of the AWS Security Hub will provide you with the tools to strengthen that defense and respond effectively to security threats.

11.1. AWS Security Hub: An Overview

AWS Security Hub is a security management system provided by Amazon Web Services (AWS) designed to simplify the management of your security and compliance. It provides a consolidated view of the high-priority security alerts and compliance status across your AWS resources.

Security Hub collects, organizes, and prioritizes security findings from across AWS services such as Amazon GuardDuty, Amazon Inspector, and Amazon Macie, and also from AWS Partner security solutions.

The Center is primarily designed to enable AWS customers to manage their security and compliance situation more easily. Instead of dealing with an inundation of individual alerts across various services, Security Hub agglomerates these alerts and findings into a single pane and helps you visually breakdown the intricate details.

11.2. Understanding Security Findings

A security finding is the AWS Security Hub term for any issue detected by one of the product integrations or the AWS-native security services. A finding includes metadata about the issue, including affected resources, the level of severity, and the account that generated the finding.

Findings are identified and categorized according to their nature, severity, and impact, allowing organizations to prioritize their responses. Whether it's unauthorized access attempts, potential data leakage, or vulnerable software, AWS Security Hub takes these findings and consolidates them into navigable, insightful data points.

11.3. Prioritizing Security Alerts

One of the core functionalities of AWS Security Hub is to help organizations prioritize their security alerts. Through AWS Security Hub, high-priority alerts are highlighted, enabling members of the organization to quickly address these concerns.

The security alerts are also visualized through integrated dashboards that allow you to see an overview of the current state of your infrastructure. These dashboards highlight any ongoing threats, vulnerabilities within your system, and any ongoing compliance issues.

11.4. Roles of AWS Security Hub

1. **Advanced Threat Detection:** Leveraging the built-in threat detection concepts from resources such as GuardDuty and Inspector, AWS Security Hub provides constant surveillance of your network and system activity. Unusual behaviors or non-

compliant activities are rapidly identified and reported back to the Security Hub for assessment.

2. **Compliance Checks:** Security Hub regularly performs automated compliance checks based on industry standards and best practices. The results of these checks fuel a comprehensive picture of an organization's overall compliance status.

3. **Aggregation and Consolidation:** A pivotal role of AWS Security Hub is to provide a central point to manage and communicate with other services. It consumes a plethora of data from many security resources, both AWS-native and partner solutions, to keep an up-to-date spectrum of your security posture.

4. **Triage and Investigation Support:** When findings occur, Security Hub supports a streamlined process for investigating and rectifying security threats. It collates and organizes the data while providing the functionality to navigate around the findings effectively.

5. **Automated Remediation:** With AWS Security Hub, you're not just pinpointing abnormalities or violations; the platform can be set to respond autonomously to specific issues, dramatically accelerating the remediation process.

11.5. Enabling AWS Security Hub

To start reaping the benefits of AWS Security Hub, it needs to be enabled within your AWS accounts. Each account independently enables Security Hub, regardless of whether the accounts are part of AWS Organizations. Once enabled, Security Hub starts consuming and analyzing data immediately.

Overall, the importance of AWS Security Hub cannot be overstated. It simplifies and streamlines security management, providing centralized visibility into your security and compliance status in the AWS environment. It identifies, organizes, and prioritizes security findings, making it simpler for you to identify and manage potential threats and vulnerabilities effectively. Through AWS Security Hub, you are able to streamline your threat detection and response mechanisms, thereby enhancing your overall security posture.

Chapter 12. Next Steps with AWS Security Hub: Extending and Optimizing your Security Operations

Once you have a foundational understanding and initial engagement with AWS Security Hub, it becomes necessary to explore further, delve into additional functionalities, and implement an extension and optimization strategy for your security operations. This chapter aims to equip you with next-level knowledge and tactics to fully leverage the AWS Security Hub and include it seamlessly into your operational landscape.

12.1. Extending AWS Security Hub Beyond Defaults

While AWS Security Hub comes with a wide array of built-in features and tools, it's highly customizable and its functionality can be extended with additional bespoke solutions. These make it possible for organizations to create security measures that align precisely with their operational needs and regulatory requirements.

To make AWS Security Hub adapt to your unique security landscape, you can design additional custom insight rules and actions. Custom insights allow you to create your own tailored search queries which facilitate unusual or case-specific event hunting, while custom actions let you respond to findings in a way that suits your specific protocols.

To create a custom insight, navigate to the Insights tab, click Create insight, and fill in your query. Remember, it's critical to encode your insight accurately to ensure the utility and accuracy of the results.

Further, AWS Security Hub can be extended beyond its out-of-the-box capabilities by integrating it with other AWS services or third party applications. Two principal ways to do so are through Amazon CloudWatch and AWS Lambda.

1. **Amazon CloudWatch:** You can configure CloudWatch Event Rule to send all AWS Security Hub findings to CloudWatch. This integration provides a unified dashboard for viewing and monitoring of all the security events.

2. **AWS Lambda:** AWS Lambda can be used to automate responses to certain Security Hub findings. You can script Lambda functions to respond to security alerts as they arise, effectively automating parts of incident response protocol.

12.2. Optimizing Your Security Operations with AWS Security Hub

Having strategies in place for optimizing your use of AWS Security Hub can further enhance your security operations. The following are some key practices:

1. **Consolidate Accounts**: AWS Security Hub is designed with multi-account functionality. Combining multiple accounts can give you a more comprehensive picture of your security landscape across various AWS accounts. You can enable AWS Security Hub for your organization either from the AWS Security Hub console or programmatically through the EnableSecurityHub operation.

2. **Use Resources Intelligently**: AWS Security Hub makes use of AWS-native resources such as AWS Config, Amazon Macie, and Amazon GuardDuty, among others. Understanding and optimizing the utilization of these resources can save costs and improve efficiency. For example, AWS Config allows for the

auditing and evaluating of configurations, offering a deeper understanding of your AWS resource inventory.

3. **Establish Proper Key Management**: Managing encryption keys is crucial when dealing with sensitive data on AWS. AWS Key Management Service (KMS) interfaces smoothly with AWS Security Hub, allowing for easy creation, control, and rotation of encryption keys used to secure your data.

4. **Continual Analysis and Improvement**: Tracking changes, evaluating findings, tweaking configurations, and adjusting settings regularly should become best practice. This practice ensures the security measures remain accurate, up-to-date, and fit for purpose, enabling your security infrastructure to evolve as cyber threats morph.

12.3. Leveraging AWS Reports and Recommendations

AWS Security Hub generates comprehensive reports and offers recommendations for security improvements, reducing the time spent on undifferentiated heavy lifting in interpreting findings.

To access this feature, select the relevant security standard from the Standards tab in AWS Security Hub. Here, you will see a detailed compliance status and recommendation report. This assists in better understanding your security posture and informs decision making on potential adjustments.

Bear in mind to set up appropriate notification protocols, alerts, and event-driven responses to make the best use of these features and ensure pristine security conditions within your AWS environment.

AWS Security Hub's capabilities, combined with a solid strategy to extend and optimize these, can significantly enhance the performance and security posture of your AWS infrastructure.

Mastery over these advanced topics will not only spill into the strengthening of your overall security operations but also provide the organization with an added layer of cyber resilience and robustness against evolving threats.

Continual exploration of AWS Security Hub's resources and making informed decisions, based on findings and recommendations, leads to iterative improvements in your security architecture. Thus, embedding these practices within your organization's security culture reaps extensive benefits - ensuring a secured, resilient, and future-proof cloud infrastructure.